# Master your destiny:

## A mindfulness-based meaning workbook

Pninit Russo-Netzer, Ph.D, &

Itai Ivtzan, Ph.D.

# Contents

**About the Authors**

# Introduction

What is your 'why'?

Throughout the history of humanity, people have been extensively preoccupied with questions such as: Why are we here? What is my purpose? What is the meaning of life?

These universal questions deal with the core concern of what it means to be human, and have inspired various myths, religions, arts, and philosophies in different cultures around the world and across time and traditions. Today, in an age of technology, instability, and constant change, these questions seem more relevant and pressing than ever. The science of meaning seeks to answer such questions. Knowing your meaning and purpose, your "why", can serve as a compass with which to navigate your life journey.

A substantial body of research in positive and existential psychology has revealed that people experiencing high levels of personal meaning are happier and more grateful, passionate, and kind. The call for meaning is sometimes like a whisper and sometimes like a shout. Being mindful allows us to notice the whispers, the subtle messages in our lives.

But what does 'meaning in life' actually mean? It has nothing to do with the meaning OF life which refers to all human beings and is a theological or philosophical question. Meaning IN life refers to your personal experience of meaning. In other words, we don't necessarily need to understand the meaning of life in general or the ultimate meaning to discover meaning in life—that which is present in every single moment in our lives.

# About this workbook

The Mindfulness-Based Meaning Program (MBMP) was created with a simple and yet transformative intention - to allow you to engage with one of the most important questions in human life: "Why are you here?" According to psychological research, being able to find a clear answer to this question will transform your life. Empirical research is discovering the many positive psychological, spiritual, and physical effects of meaning, from academic achievement and occupational success to coping with life's adversities, happiness, life satisfaction, and physical health. We created this workbook program to help you find your personal meaning and purpose in life.

The Mindfulness-Based Meaning Program (MBMP) is the first comprehensive program to bring these two important aspects of well-being together—meaning in life and mindfulness. As part of this program, we use mindfulness as a spotlight to shed light on our past meaningful moments, our present experience of meaning in the here and now, and our potential purpose in the future that will provide us with a deep sense of meaning. With mindfulness, it becomes easier to see all of these and to create a clear understanding of your meaning and purpose.

The journey to discover your meaning and purpose, might not be an easy one—but we will offer you a series of theories, activities, and exercises that will provide you with all the support you need to help you answer this question (i.e., "Why are you here?") and find your personal meaning and purpose in life. Our workbook program is unique because it is completely research-based. Every theory, exercise, and topic we teach has been researched and found to be effective in increasing our experience of meaning and purpose. This program is also unique as it brings together two main evidence-based fields—meaning in life and mindfulness.

Finally, the workbook includes downloadable meditations that accompany your learning journey and support your growth. At any section of the book in which you are invited to download a meditation you will find this QR code below, scan it to download (for free) this support content:

## Why knowing our purpose is important

When we think about flourishing and living life fully, we can focus on two groups of people. The first consists of those who wake up in the morning with a clear sense of knowledge of their "why"—they know why they get out of bed. The second consists of those who are confused or uncertain as to their "why —they don't have a clear answer as to why they should get out of bed in the morning. This answer to the "why" of your life has a tremendous impact on your well-being. It leads to passion, vitality, enthusiasm, and fills you with a sense of purpose and direction. You could use these feelings as an indicator of whether you are living your meaning. For example, when you are living your meaning, you may have more enthusiasm and passion because you are devoting your time to "what really matters."

When we have no knowledge of our personal meaning (our 'why'), then we may experience confusion when making choices, which may lead us to choose irrelevant, false, or empty experiences. A classic example is an irrelevant and empty job, or even a sense of existential vacuum, boredom, emptiness, or anxiety that might lead to addictions. On the other hand, having a clear meaning and purpose makes it much easier to make choices because if you know your personal meaning, your purpose, all you need to ask yourself is whether or not a certain opportunity, a particular option, is aligned with that knowledge.

And this is when mindfulness becomes essential for our journey toward meaning and purpose. As previously mentioned, using mindfulness as a spotlight to identify past meaningful moments, experience meaning in the present, and uncover potential purpose in the future provides us with a deep sense of meaning. Mindfulness makes it easier to see all of these and helps us to create a clear understanding of our meaning and purpose.

# Packing our backpack for the journey of mindfulness and meaning

Because this is the first comprehensive program that brings together both meaning and mindfulness, it offers a unique, integrative, and deeper experience of meaning. During this workbook program, we will show you how mindfulness makes it easier to find and strengthen the building blocks of your personal meaning in life.

How does the program work? Like any other journey, there might be places where you wish to stop, breathe, and enjoy the scenery, while in other places you might move faster, and that's perfectly natural. Whatever pace you choose, think about this program as an adventure, an internal treasure hunt where you move deeper into yourself. It's one of the most beautiful and beneficial treasures you could find.

We invite you now to begin the journey of deepening your personal meaning and purpose by completing the first exercise of the program. In this exercise, you will be establishing your goal for the workbook program.

## Exercise 1: Calibrating your Compass

Like a physical journey, using a compass can show you where your personal "north" is and the direction you are heading. Psychological research shows that setting a clear goal at the beginning of a program increases our dedication, engagement, motivation, and the positive impacts of this workbook program.

To help calibrate your compass and set your goals for the program, please reflect on the following questions:

- What brought you to this program? Why have you decided to join it?

- What would you like to achieve on this program?

- What could help you fulfil your goal in everyday life?

- What time constraints do you foresee and how can you plan around them to ensure consistent engagement with the program?

# Exercise 2: Transcending the Boundaries of your Comfort Zone

With any journey, it is natural for us to have certain patterns that might hold us back in some ways. These could be, for instance, negative previous experiences, negative thoughts, or simply fear of the unknown. For this reason, it is important for us to recognize these patterns so that we are aware of the potential impact they may have while on our journey and arriving at our destination.

Let's begin by clarifying three potential zones in which we handle ourselves and our lives:

- **Comfort zone**: a place, situation, or mental state where we feel safe, or at ease, but often disengaged as there is little stimulus or anxiety to drive change.

- **Courage or 'learning' zone**: the area outside the comfort zone, here there is just enough stimulus and anxiety to drive productivity and flow.

- **Panic zone**: an area furthest away from the comfort zone, here there is too much stimulus and/or anxiety, which can often lead to a decline in productivity.

For instance, consider public speaking. An experienced speaker might automatically feel they are in their comfort zone, however, to increase stimulus, they may need a new topic, more crowds, or being videoed to move them into their courage zone. On the other hand, an inexperienced speaker might automatically find themselves in their panic zone, and therefore need to reduce stimulus by choosing a venue with a smaller crowd, a familiar topic, and by practicing frequently to move into their courage zone.

- Look at the three circles below. In the context of your journey ahead, reflect on your goal (as you did in the previous exercise) and explore its ingredients.

- What behavior, thoughts, emotions, and activities are reflected in your goal?

- Write down each ingredient in the most relevant circle below (one of the three).

- Which ingredients in the comfort and panic zone could move you into the courage zone? How would you do this?

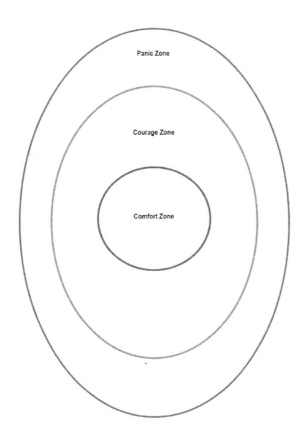

Panic Zone

Courage Zone

Comfort Zone

## Exercise 3: Getting Ready for the Journey

Your journey toward personal meaning and purpose is about to begin. As with any journey, you will need to pack the resources you will require along the way. It may be helpful to consider any ingredients you listed in previous exercise.

A.  What would you take in your backpack on this journey for meaning so that it will be a fulfilling one? What characteristics, skills, qualities, and strengths would you include? For example, you could bring your curiosity, passion, enthusiasm, wisdom, life experience, love of learning, and anything else that is part of you and could support you on this journey. Make a list that includes as many of these as possible.

B. In addition, what resources, people, and conditions in your life might support you on this journey? For example, there may be certain people in your life who would be particularly helpful. There might be specific days/time-slots in your week when you are completely free and could dedicate time to this journey. There might be other activities, such as courses you are taking, that might be useful. Make a list that includes as many of these as possible.

# Embarking on the journey: Meaning in life

*"There is a vitality, a life force, an energy, a quickening that is translated through you into action, and because there is only one of you in all of time, this expression is unique."* --Martha Graham

## Exercise 4: Exploration of Meaning

Let's start unpacking the concept of meaning in life by first exploring your personal definition of meaning.

1.  What is meaning? What is meant by meaning? What comes to mind when you think about the word "meaning"?

2.  Once you have written your definition of meaning, try to create or find an image or text that represents what meaning means to you. This can be an image, a picture, a quote, or whatever you feel best captures the essence of what meaning means to you.

3.  Why did you choose this particular image or quote? What is it about this image or quote that aligns with your idea of meaning?

Throughout the history of humanity, people have been extensively preoccupied with existential questions, such as: Why are we here? What is my purpose? What do I stand for? What is the meaning of life? Who am I? Does my life matter?

As far as we know, animals, computers, or machines do not ask such questions. They are not concerned with why they are here or working out the purpose of their existence. These universal questions are essentially and uniquely human. They touch the core of our existence as human beings and have been pursued through history and across cultures. They have inspired various myths, religions, arts, and philosophies in different cultures around the world and across time and traditions.

Today, in an age of knowledge explosion, uncertainties, individualism, and technology where "better, faster, higher" are sacred values—the void left by the collapse of stable structures and binding values emphasizes the need for an anchor, a 'lighthouse' to navigate our life journeys. Meaning in life can serve as a 'lighthouse', shedding light on our life experiences, and providing a sense of purpose, direction, and a feeling that things matter. It is the essential organizing principle in our lives. In other words, meaning in life involves the feeling that our lives matter, are coherent (logically fit together or make sense to you), and are directed toward a purpose or a broader mission.

These essential principles correspond to three main conceptual components that researchers have highlighted as the building blocks of the definition of meaning in life, they include: **Comprehension** (the cognitive component), which is the ability to understand and make sense of your life experiences and weave them into a coherent whole; **Purpose** (the motivational component), which is the degree to which you feel directed and motivated by valued life goals; and **Mattering** (the existential-emotional component), which is the belief that your existence is significant and valued.

Now that we have looked at the definition of meaning, it is useful to discuss why meaning in life is so important. What is it good for? Well, curiously, although our culture is occupied with the pursuit of happiness, recent studies that have taken a closer look at such a pursuit have found that it might have some negative effects. And even when it is achieved, such happiness is frequently short lived. The pursuit of meaning, on the other hand, has been found to contribute to lasting and deeper wellbeing. A great example of this is the distinction we make in positive psychology between hedonic and eudaimonic well-being. Hedonic wellbeing is all about feeling good, positive emotions, feeling more pleasure. So, if your boss says something nice to you, or if you are given a raise, if you eat a wonderful piece of chocolate cake, this is where you feel hedonically wonderful. It feels really good, right? While the feeling is short lived, it is an important part of our well-being.

Eudaimonic well-being is a very different experience. It is not a short-lived experience, instead it is a long process, a journey, where we integrate our positive and negative emotions and experiences. And at the heart of that journey is meaning in life, through which we navigate our eudaimonic well-being, inviting more growth, greater self-discovery, and deeper and lasting well-being. Psychological research indicates that meaning is important to our well-being and is linked to our ability to cope with difficulties, to be more resilient, and to thrive in life. It has been found to be linked to better mental and physical health, including our longevity.

Viktor Frankl, an Austrian psychiatrist, neurologist, and Holocaust survivor, founded a branch of existential analysis known as logotherapy, a meaning-focused approach to therapy, and is well known for being the first to refer to meaning as the primary motivating force in humans. This idea, encapsulated in the phrase 'will to meaning' goes beyond Freud's 'will to pleasure' or Adler's 'will to power.' In this context, Frankl once said, "I would not be willing to live merely for the sake of my defense mechanisms, nor would I be ready to die merely for the sake of my reaction formations. Humans, however, are able to live and even to die for the sake of their ideals and values." This attitude to life was put to the test during World War II where, in the darkness of oppression and physical and psychological deprivation, Frankl experienced in himself and in others an inner spark, a force by which he was able to rise above suffering and despair and choose to take a stand, to embrace and fulfil human potential. That choice fills life with meaning, for without it, we would have no vision or hope for the future, no possibility of growth or change. This is because without meaning there would be nothing to arouse, evoke, or motivate us, and no passion that could inspire and energize us to move forward.

Throughout this workbook, we will take a closer look at our meaningful moments and experiences in the past, the potential that lies in living the meaning of the moment in the present, and the legacy and purpose we wish to leave behind when looking toward the future. This journey entails self-reflection, self-discovery, and sometimes self-acceptance and self-compassion. If we can understand ourselves more deeply through self-care and self-awareness, we can create greater interconnectedness between the various parts of our being: body, mind, and spirit. When we observe our meaningful moments in the past, realize the potential of meaning in the present moment, and look forward to our future purpose, that is where mindfulness is essential. Mindfulness provides us with the clarity to observe the past, present, and future in a healthy manner so that we can derive as much meaning as possible from all of them. Mindfulness thus becomes our 'lighthouse', illuminating deeper meaning in our lives.

# Exercise 5: Become a Meaning Detective

To find meaning in our lives, we first need to notice meaningful moments. Doing so can offer us insight into the personal meaning that is contained in different situations and aspects of our lives. During this exercise, you will become a 'meaning detective,' that is, you will mindfully look for meaning as you go through your day. You will be searching for meaningful moments—identifying activities, encounters, and situations that bring meaning to your life. For example, you may identify moments of meaning with your friends or parent or child; you may realize a moment of meaning in a song played on the radio or on your mobile device; you may detect a moment of meaning in nature during sunrise or sunset; or you may identify a moment of meaning during your day at work. These could be found as part of the "big" or "small", "joyful" or "sad", and "beautiful" or "ugly" moments in life. All it takes is for you to pay attention and notice those meaningful moments—for this reason, you are now taking on the role of a "meaning detective." As part of this practice, let go of skepticism, which might obstruct the identification of moments of meaning, by saying, "true, but… this isn't big enough or important enough to be considered meaningful."

During the next few days, using the detective's magnifying glass, notice and write down as many meaningful moments, derived from as many sources as possible in your life. To "notice" means recognizing the actual moments where meaning is present.

Examples of noticing include nature-oriented experiences, interactions with people, situations at work, and engaging with arts.

For each of those meaningful moments you notice, write down what has been captured as part of that moment. To "capture" means identifying the qualities involved in the meaningful moment that has been noticed. Such capturing will include your emotions, thoughts, bodily sensations, and insights.

Using the two images below as a metaphor, where the magnifying glass represents what you "noticed" and the butterfly net is what you "captured" an example might be:

1. You **noticed** a meaningful sunset (the magnifying glass image) and **captured** serenity, beauty, and peace (the butterfly net image).

2. You **noticed** a meaningful conversation with your mother (the magnifying glass image) and **captured** compassion and caring (the butterfly net image).

Looking at your list of noticed meaningful moments and their captured qualities, what have you learned about yourself and about meaning in your life?

# Exercise 6: Strengthening the Meaning Muscle

In positive psychology, character strengths refer to a list of positive human traits that direct our emotions, thoughts, and behavior while providing a sense of purpose and meaning. In the following exercise, you will identify and reflect your own personal strengths in the context of meaning.

First, please identify your strengths by taking the free character strengths survey (from VIA). You can find the survey by going to the VIA website:

https://www.viacharacter.org/survey/Account/Register

Once you receive your results, reflect on your top five strengths to answer the questions below:

1. How do your top five strengths relate to your experience of meaning in life?

2. For example, as part of Exercise 1, you may have noticed different meaningful moments during your time in nature, and, for example, captured peace, awe, and beauty as part of the experience. In your list of top five strengths, you may have written "appreciation of beauty" which could easily relate to and reflect the meaning you found earlier.

3. Now, choose one strength from your list of top five strengths, and practice applying it during the activities you identified as meaningful in Exercise 1. Please make sure

this is a new strength, one you have not applied before to this meaningful experience. For example, in your previous meaningful experience of nature, other than "appreciation of beauty", you could apply the strength of "curiosity" or "gratitude" to enrich and deepen the meaning experienced.

# Embarking on the journey: Mindfulness

What is Mindfulness? There are many, many ways to approach it, to think about it, and to define it. But we invite you to think about it in a very simple manner. Think about mindfulness as any moment when the activity and your mind are one. In other words, any moment where what you do and where your mind is are interconnected. Too often, our activity and our mind are in different places. For example, when we drink a cup of tea, and the activity—drinking tea—is inviting us to feel the taste and to smell the tea, but our mind is thinking about completely different things—say the fact that we need to wash the dishes. And then when we are washing the dishes, there is another invitation for us to be in the present moment by feeling the texture of the water or the temperature of the water, but again, our mind is moving somewhere else. This creates a duality—a never-ending cycle of doing something while being within our minds somewhere else. And it is this duality we are trying to disrupt through the practice of mindfulness. When we bring the activity and mind together, we practice mindfulness. When we drink that tea, for example, we really notice the smells and the tastes, and when we are in a conversation with someone, we are present, connected, and engaged. We are really there with the other person.

Mindfulness Meditation is one of the most popular exercises when it comes to psychology and well-being. The reason for this is that we now have an extensive body of scientific research that is growing with every passing year. Whereas 20 or 30 years ago, we may have been asking questions about mindfulness, whether it is as impactful as we think, and whether it's really going to help us, now there are no doubts. We know how effective mindfulness is. Through research and science, we know that, for example, it has a really strong impact on a physiological level, affecting blood pressure, heart rate, and hypertension. All are reduced as a result of the practice of mindfulness. It is also helpful in the treatment of disease. When combining mindfulness with traditional therapy for diabetes and cancer, you get much better results. There is also a variety of psychological elements that are improved as a result of the practice of mindfulness. Yet all of those benefits are the results of regular practice, not a one-off session, but a consistent habit. When we do practice regularly, we improve our concentration. Our attention and concentration increase, we sleep better, and our anxiety and stress levels decrease. Our happiness, hope, and gratitude increase.

When we think about mindfulness, it is important to distinguish between formal and informal practice. Because often we think of mindfulness as something we do outside our everyday lives—where we sit rigidly, with a straight back, hands resting on our knees, eyes closed, and observing our breath. That is the formal practice of mindfulness and it is very helpful. However, we can also take part in an informal practice where we integrate mindfulness into any moment in life. Remember that activity and mind brought together equals mindfulness? So when you are in the shower and you really notice the temperature of the water that is touching your body and how it feels, or you notice the fragrance of the soap and shampoo, you are practicing mindfulness. When you are running or walking and you feel your muscles, the sweat dripping your face, then you are being mindful. If we do not let our mind wander, and instead really try to connect to the present moment of the experience of showering, running, walking, or any activity you do, we are practicing mindfulness.

Studies show that washing the dishes can be a really good invitation for mindfulness. Notice the temperature of the water, the liquid soap, and the texture of the plate, and you are practicing mindfulness. This is a really relevant point when it comes to our journey. Throughout the program, we will be inviting you to become aware of that meaning and purpose in your everyday activities, in order for you to deepen your experience of meaning and purpose. Instead of thinking about mindfulness as something you have to devote time to outside of your daily activities, we invite you to think about it as something that could be integrated into (pretty much) anything you do! This leads to greater self-awareness. When we are present in those different activities, in those different moments, when we engage with other people, we learn about ourselves. We learn who we are and what we are made out of—and that is the heart and soul of this journey. The Mindfulness-based Meaning Program is based on that experience of "know thyself." Knowing yourself better, increases self-awareness, which will deepen your meaning and purpose in life.

Mindfulness enables us to deepen our experience of meaning on two complementary levels. The first is our larger-scale understanding of meaning in life, which answers the question, "Why am I here?" The second is the moment-to-moment experience of meaning in our daily lives—the meaning of the moment. Building a foundation of mindfulness can help you use mindfulness a resource throughout your journey to find meaning and purpose in your own life. However, mindfulness is a skill, like riding a bicycle, and like any skill, is a matter of practicing until you know the way it works and how to apply it. Think about mindfulness as a skill that strengthens itself through practice, just like any other muscle that you develop and strengthen through physical practice.

There are number of mindfulness myths that we need to discuss first. The first is the idea that mindfulness is practiced sitting rigidly. As mentioned earlier, mindfulness could be practiced as part of any daily activity: walking, running, taking a shower, eating, washing the dishes, gardening; whatever you do, mindfulness could be part of it. The second myth is the idea that mindfulness is easy. Now, mindfulness could be easy some days and quite challenging on others. It depends on how hectic your mind is on a particular day as you sit and meditate; hence, it fluctuates and moves through time.

Another myth is the idea that mindfulness feels great, that it is a joyful experience. Mindfulness can be joyful; it can be a positive thing that is moving within us, but it can also be an uncomfortable experience. Mindfulness basically engages you with yourself. Mindfulness is where you stop distracting yourself from whatever is going on and move inside yourself to start noticing. Then you will notice some things that will feel great and some other things that won't feel that nice, but whatever you engage with, whatever you notice, it is really important for your psychological well-being.

Another myth is the idea that mindfulness is passive. People may say, "well, this mindfulness stuff, it's all very interesting, but I'm afraid of becoming like a couch potato or becoming a passive person." Well, it is important here not to confuse the idea of something that is restful with mindfulness. Mindfulness is indeed restful, but instead of becoming passive, it fills us with vitality and zest. Mindfulness will not turn you into someone who is passive—you will be filled with that energy and enthusiasm. This is a part of the process of the practice.

Lastly, the final myth to challenge is the idea that mindfulness is about stopping our thoughts. Some people try to practice mindfulness and they realize, "hmm I'm still thinking," as a result, they think that they have failed. Absolutely not. With mindfulness, we are not trying to stop our thoughts. The mind will keep on producing thoughts. We are, however, changing our relationship with our thoughts. And there is a big difference between these two ideas. Mindfulness enables us to move from a relationship that is filled with attachment and reaction—where, whatever we think about or whatever you feel, we are immediately swept away into a relationship with those thoughts and feelings—into a relationship, where we can observe more peacefully in a non-reactive manner, our thoughts and feelings. These are fundamentally different relationships with whatever is going on in our minds.

You are now going to practice a number of mindfulness exercises. You might find them enjoyable and you might find them challenging. Whichever it is, remember they are fundamental to your journey as part of this exploration of personal meaning and purpose.

## Exercise 7: Pit Stop (1): Connecting with Yourself through Mindful Breath

The first mindfulness exercise is a mediation to help you to connect with yourself through your breath. Download the meditation onto your computer or mobile phone and practice at any time that is convenient to you. Practice at least once. To download the meditation script or listen to a guided mindful breathing meditation use this QR code:

Alternatively, you can find the meditation script of the Breathing Meditation at the end of this workbook.

After completing each meditation practice, dedicate a few minutes to reflect on and answer the following questions:

- How was the mindfulness meditation practice for you today? What did you notice?

- Have you learned anything about yourself from the practice? Try to find something, even if it is a very minor detail (e.g., you may find it easier to relax in your garden than in your living room; you may feel your lungs filling today very clearly; you may have an internal feeling of sadness that you were not aware of before the practice).

## Exercise 8: Pit Stop (2): Connecting with Yourself through your Body

Similar to the previous exercise, this mindfulness exercise is a mediation to help you to connect with yourself, this time through your body. You can download the meditation onto your computer or mobile phone and practice at any time that is convenient to you. Practice at least once. To download the meditation script or listen to a guided mindful breathing meditation use this QR code:

Alternatively, you can find the meditation script of the Body-Scan Meditation at the end of this workbook.

After completing each meditation practice, dedicate a few minutes to reflect on and answer the following questions:

– How was the practice of the mindfulness meditation today?

– Have you learned anything about yourself from the practice? Try to find something, even if it is a very minor detail (e.g., you may feel tightening around your chest;

your heart may feel open and light; your body may feel energized/sluggish).

## Exercise 9: Gratitude Meditation

As we prepare for our meaning meditations, we create a meditative foundation. We started with our breath, explored our body, and now we are going to lay the foundation of meditative gratitude. Similar to the previous exercise, this mindfulness exercise is a mediation to help you to connect with yourself, this time through gratitude. You can download the meditation onto your computer or mobile phone and practice at any time that is convenient to you. Practice at least once. To download the meditation script or listen to a guided mindful breathing meditation use this QR code:

Alternatively, you can find the meditation script of the Gratitude Meditation at the end of this workbook.

After completing each meditation practice, dedicate a few minutes to reflect on and answer the following questions:

- How was the practice of the mindfulness meditation today?

- Have you learned anything about yourself from the practice? Try to find something, even if it is a very minor detail (e.g., you may feel tightening around your chest; your heart may feel open and light; your body may feel energized/sluggish).

## Exercise 10: Hitting Mindful Roots

The aim of this exercise is to help you better understand your 'mindful roots', that is, a place where you feel at 'home' and more easily connect with. Choose one of the three mindfulness meditations you have been practicing (breathing body-scan, and gratitude), the one that felt most natural for you. For the next week, practice it once every day. If it feels right turn it into a daily habit.

At the end of each day, answer the following questions:

1. What did you notice in your meditation today?

2. Did it influence your day in any way?

# Sources of Meaning

Let's take a closer look at how meaning plays out in your life. Steve Jobs, the co-founder of Apple is remembered for his timeless commencement speech at Stanford University where he told his life story and summarized it by saying: "you cannot connect the dots looking forward. You can only connect the dots looking backwards. So you have to trust that the dots will somehow connect in your future. You have to trust in something, your gut, destiny, life, karma, whatever. This approach has never let me down and it has made all the difference in my life." As Steve Jobs said, connecting the dots is essential for a personal understanding of meaning, but in order to connect the dots, we first need to highlight and acknowledge each and every one of them.

## Exercise 11: Connecting the Dots: Identifying Meaning in your Life Story

The purpose of this exercise is to identify meaning (your dots) within your life story. Looking back at your life's journey thus far, write a couple of paragraphs about meaningful crossroads and the choices you made.

In this next step, you will create a word cloud to 'analyze' your story. To do this, go to the Word Clouds website (http://www.wordclouds.com/), then, select "Wizard" (which gives you a tour of the functions within the app). To bypass the tour, you can select, "Word List" and "Use the Paste/Type text dialog" to quickly access the dialogue box. Lastly, paste the paragraph you wrote in the previous step into the dialog box.

If you experience any issues with this website, you can try an alternative one: https://monkeylearn.com/word-cloud/ then paste your paragraph into the dialogue box.

Save your word cloud—your life's work of art—and 'analyze' the words that are given greater prominence. Are there words which appear more frequently in your text?

- What can you learn from it?

- Can you identify any sources of meaning in your life?

The activity you've just completed took you closer to understanding your own sources of meaning. Sources of meaning can be anything (a memory, an object, a physical place, an experience) that we feel is 'meaningful' to us. When we explore empirical research on sources of meaning, we discover that they fall into four different categories. The **first category** is sources of meaning that take us beyond our personal needs and interests, such as connections to a higher power or contributing to a greater good or cause greater than yourself. The **second category** is sources of meaning that include fulfillment of our potential, which means getting to know your own values and abilities, and then living according to those. The **third category** concerns sources of meaning which relate to belonging, being part of something, something cultural, ethnic, religious; certain traditions, for example, that are meaningful to you. This provides a sense of order in our lives. The **final category** is sources of meaning that provide us with pleasure, connection, and a sense of well-being, which can be experienced both alone and in the company of others.

Research has shown that not all these sources are equal in their impact. For instance, having goals oriented beyond our personal needs and interests is more likely to yield an experience of meaning. It is also important to consider the diversity and prominence of sources of meaning. Diversity is having different and varied sources of meaning; which can then act as a buffer. So, in circumstances where a certain source of meaning is threatened by life events, other sources of meaning can still provide meaning to your life and compensate. For example, if work is a prominent source of meaning for you and you are being told you might be fired, having other sources of meaning, such as a supportive family or volunteering in a meaningful place, can compensate for the temporary loss of work as a source of meaning in life. This is called the 'fluid compensation model' in psychology, which captures our ability to adjust to changing life circumstances. In essence, we can derive meaning from different sources of meaning.

In this context, relationships and connectedness play a key role in the experience and fostering of meaning in life. A sense of relatedness includes various types of connections, such as those with other people, with society as a whole, with nature, and with a transcendent power. People who perceive themselves as part of a group report a higher sense of fulfillment, whereas people who perceive themselves to be socially excluded report a loss of meaning. Relationships not only give us a sense of belonging, but also form a crucial part of our identity and self-esteem. We can also see the importance of social ties with regard to meaning from an evolutionary perspective. The most dominant form of relatedness associated with a meaningful life is family, which spans various age groups and cultures. Another important aspect to consider is the effect of cognition, which refers to the impact of thought processes on our life story. We use our memories within our daily lives to form a script which consists of information about sequences of events and the linkages that bind them together. It is this script we use when we combine our memories and experiences into a coherent life story.

Constructing our life story is a delicate art of integrating different aspects of life: the highs and lows, losses and triumphs, joy and pain, light and shadow. Indeed, people are able to derive meaning from both positive and negative events in their life story. Let's start with the positive. Studies reveal that our current mood in any given situation can be used as an unconscious source of information when making judgements. For example, one study reported that satisfaction with life was rated higher on sunny days. Positive emotion has been shown to facilitate creative problem-solving, broaden the scope of attention, and increase openness to processing new types of information and cognitive flexibility. When people are able to think more broadly, they are more likely to perceive meaning in their daily existence as part of a greater system of meaning. But meaning can also be found, not only through the positive, but also unpleasant or negative events. Finding meaning within negative life events has proven to be a powerful coping mechanism, helping us adapt, and move forward following a difficulty. Lack of control and predictability in our lives is a major contributor to stress. Creating an inner process that gives us a sense of control reduces that stress. Finding meaning in negative events is an inner process that gives us that feeling of control. Studies support this notion, revealing that a sense of meaning not only lowers stress, but also serves as a buffer against anticipated stress. By giving negative events meaning, people are able to view the events as something that made sense in the context of their story. This is so important. The idea that whatever you go through, however challenging it is, is something you understand. It makes sense to you in the context of your personal story. In this way, you can accept difficulties and stress as challenges rather than threats. In Frankl's words, "human life can be fulfilled not only by creating and enjoying, but also in suffering." As we can see, our life story includes both the positive and the negative. Both add to our sense of meaning in life.

## Exercise 12: Discovering your Life's Lesson

Begin with a reflection on this question: If your entire life had been designed in advance to enable you to learn something from it, what would be the lesson you were supposed to have learned?

## Exercise 13: Connecting Life Events: Mindful Meaning through challenges

Mindfulness exercise: Research shows that life's challenges frequently carry a sense of meaning for us. While pushing our boundaries and being unpleasant, they are also triggering and expanding our sense of meaning.

In this guided meditation you are invited to engage with a challenge in your life and come in touch with the meaning that it triggers within you.

To download the meditation script or listen to a guided mindful meaning through challenge meditation use this QR code:

Alternatively, you can find the meditation script of the meditation at the end of this workbook.

After completing each meditation practice, dedicate a few minutes to reflect on and answer the following questions:

1. What was your experience of this meditation?

2. In what way did the challenge and your meaning came together?

## Exercise 14: The Soundtrack of Your Life

1. Choose a meaningful song that reflects a challenging, inspiring, or transformational time in your life. Listen to it and be mindful of its meaning to you and any bodily sensations and emotions it triggers.

2. What is your 'take away' from this exercise? What insights have you found, and how do they contribute to your understanding of meaning in your life?

## Exercise 15: Scripting your Life

– Construct an outline of a movie about your life thus far. What would be the features of such a movie? (consider the genre, likely actors, title, budget, twists, favorite scenes, and ending).

– What can you learn from this exercise about central aspects of your life (you can choose to focus on any number of the following options): key experiences in life, who you are as a person, the things that are meaningful to you, your values and goals, and important relationships.

# Experiencing Meaning in your Daily Life

We have discussed our life story and what we can learn about ourselves and about meaning in life through a blend of the positive and negative. Now we will focus on the present, on being mindful to the meaning of each and every moment in our lives.

We humans do not like to think of our own mortality, but it is not the concept of death that scares us, as much as the notion that we may reach the end of our life, our last breath, and realize that we have not really, truly, fully lived; this can be a scary thought. As Elizabeth Kübler-Ross, author of *Death: The Final Stage of Growth*, puts it, "it is the denial of death that is partially responsible for people living empty purposeless lives; for when you live as if you'll live forever, it becomes too easy to postpone the things you know that you must do."

We now invite you to take part in an activity to reflect on your relationship with death. In many cultures, death is considered a key to the gate of life, a teacher of how to live life meaningfully and fully.

Please reflect on the following questions:

1. When you contemplate your own death, what do you experience? (e.g., what are your thoughts, emotions, regrets, bodily sensations, etc.).

2. What does your engagement with your future death teach you about your own meaning in life and the things that are meaningful to you?

Every situation, every unrepeatable moment in our lives offers unique meaning potential. Listening to the call of life entails paying attention and using our true self as a compass to track the power of meaning in the present moment. The call for meaning is sometimes like a whisper and sometimes like a shout. Death is an example of the strongest shout. Being mindful allows us to notice the whispers, the subtle messages in our lives. It can make us more aware and more present every day of our lives, and allow us to be grateful for life's gifts and see the potential meaning in challenging situations.

Various researchers have tried to answer the question of what makes us feel that we have lived fully. One concept that has been discussed is the distinction between a happy life and a meaningful life. A happy life is more oriented toward positive emotions and positive experiences. A meaningful life, on the other hand, is composed of both positive and negative emotions and experiences, which allows us to feel a deeper connection to life, a vital engagement. It is crucial therefore, to have not only positive life events, but to experience and overcome struggles, challenges in our environment, and in our daily lives, in order to produce an enduring sense of meaning.

Mindfulness is the tool that allows us to be here in the present moment, whether it is a joyful or difficult one, and to accept the moment as it is. Mindfulness is essential, if we want to experience the meaning that the moment offers. A powerful example of this can be found in the positive psychology concept of 'savoring.' Savoring allows us to generate, to intensify, to prolong enjoyment and appreciation; for example, when you come home in the evening from work and open the door and see your child running toward you to hug you. When we practice mindfulness, we are more mindful of the opportunity of that moment. Instead of quickly hugging him or her and moving on to your evening tasks, you become more aware of the potential of the moment and of the hidden meaning that is waiting to unravel. That hug can be felt with deep awareness, intention, and mindfulness. It may only take a few seconds, but it can transform your experience! This is an example of how savoring can be applied to find more meaning in our everyday experiences, and we need mindfulness to do that.

Meaning is waiting to be discovered in many situations and opportunities in life. Living a meaningful life is strongly related to the present moment and getting in touch with our true self. The notion of "being" is one that we have deviated from transitioning to modern society. We are so fully engaged with the "doing" of activities, with moving forward with success, which is important for our well-being, but equally important for our well-being is having a balance. We need to be able to move into being as well. It seems that we have missed that experience of being which is fundamental to living psychologically healthy and meaningful lives. Being in the present moment and allowing ourselves to experience our emotions, both the positive and the negative, in a non-judgmental manner leads to a feeling of deep meaning and peace.

Being in touch with our authentic self (or true self), the person we feel we truly are, has implications for how meaningful we perceive our lives to be. Studies suggest that people who report that their behavior typically expresses their authentic self, perceived life as more meaningful than those who do not feel they are living authentically. Finding our true self requires self-reflection, self-observation, and self awareness. With mindfulness and self-awareness, which are vital to decerning our deepest held personal values, we can then align our daily choices and activities to these values. Such an ongoing process enables individuals to shape and cultivate a sense of personal meaning which is authentic, personally relevant, and rooted in everyday experiences. This is also an important mechanism in prioritizing meaning which involves actively organizing our daily routines to include meaningful activities. Prioritizing meaning in everyday life has been found to be positively associated with life satisfaction, happiness, positive emotions, a sense of coherence, gratitude, and the experience of meaning in life.

## Exercise 16: Mindful Snapshots of Meaning

This purpose of this exercise is help you engage with life and capture how you experience meaningful moments.

- Choose between walking outside or around your home. While you are walking, take a picture of anything that triggers a feeling of meaning within you. In the next exercise you will engage with picture (meaningful snapshots).

## Exercise 17: Mindful Engagement with your Meaningful Snapshots

As a follow-up to the previous exercise, write a visual-based meditation using the image. To do this, focus on the image, taking in every possible detail, as if you have never seen this image before. For example, notice objects in the image, the colors, the shading and lighting, the composition, what stands out, what is in background, what is out of focus. Those familiar with the raisin meditation will notice the similarities. After you have taken in as many details as possible, close your eyes and feel the internal impact.

## Exercise 18: Celebrating the Time We Have

Here we engage in a thought experiment and consider our own death. The purpose of the exercise to notice changes we might experience or make as result of facing our own mortality.

Trigger warning: please note that this activity invites you to engage with the possibility of death. While this has been shown to be helpful for our relationship with meaning and purpose, it might also feel uncomfortable if you have been facing bereavement lately. Please skip this activity if it feels too much at the moment.

Imagine that you have exactly one year until your death. What changes will you make in this final year of your life in the following areas: changes to relationships, changes to lifestyle, and changes to attitude.

## Exercise 19: Sucking the Marrow out of Life

Like the previous exercise, we are again engaging in a thought-exercise considering our own death. This time you will imagine you have one week to live. For the first three days you will conduct yourself as if this is true. In addition to behaving as if you have only seven days left to live, write down during those days any insights you have concerning differences you find in your approach and interactions compared to any other day.

# Translating Meaning into Purpose and Calling

In our previous sections, we have explored ways to engage with meaning in the past and in the present. Here, we will take our next step toward meaningful living, by looking forward to the future with a sense of direction and purpose. We will begin with a brief activity which is the best possible legacy meditation. It is a meditation which combines mindfulness with meaning.

## Exercise 20: Best Legacy Meditation

When you look into the future, what would you like your legacy to be? What meaning do you infuse your future with? In this guided meditation you envision your best possible legacy, engaging with the vision of your best possible future creation. Such a creation is filled with your personal meaning and purpose.

To download the meditation script or listen to a guided best legacy meditation use this QR code:

Alternatively, you can find the meditation script of the meditation at the end of this workbook.

After completing each meditation practice, dedicate a few minutes to reflect on and answer the following questions:

1. What was your experience of this meditation?

2. What was your best legacy and which aspects of your personal meaning and purpose do you find in this legacy?

Humans by nature seek purpose. Purpose is the applied dimension of our personal meaning. It is the motivation that moves us forward to create our future and to make a difference in the world. Purpose also orients us. It provides us with a sense of direction and concentrates our energies toward a personally meaningful goal we're committed to. Strikingly, studies have shown that one of the key predictors of health and well-being in old age is whether individuals continue to have a purpose-driven life as they grow old. Adults who are concerned with leaving a legacy and taking care of future generations are healthier, more satisfied, and more resilient than other adults. Conversely, a lack of purpose has been associated with a variety of psychological difficulties such as boredom, an existential vacuum, depression, anxiety, and hopelessness. Having a sense of direction, a sense of purpose, is an essential ingredient of a meaningful life.

It is important, though, to differentiate between goals that are driven by our environment and goals that are driven by our true self. In order to experience a deep sense of meaning, we need to feel that different aspects of ourselves are coherent. For example, if your goal is to be effective and successful, but not aligned with your true self, this will result in a feeling of discomfort. It would not feel authentic. You may feel an uncomfortable feeling in the pit of your stomach. People experience greater meaning not only when they are doing well, but also when what they are doing reflects their authentic self-identity. A worthwhile goal engages emotional, cognitive, and physical aspects of our being and also seeks accomplishments in meaningful life domains. In the words of Maslow, "a musician must make music. An artist must paint. A poet must write if he is to be ultimately at peace with himself. What a man can be, he must be."

The idea of having a purpose is strongly related to a sense of calling. A sense of calling is feeling guided by a force outside ourselves to help others or to do work for the greater good. Studies have demonstrated that higher levels of calling in relation to one's work links to higher levels of psychological well-being. Research on work orientation suggests people can derive meaning from almost any type of work, depending on how they relate to and approach their work. Studies indicate that people tend to frame this relationship in three potential ways: as a job, a career, or a calling. People who view work as a job tend to focus on its financial value and explore their interests outside of work. People who view their work as a career tend to seek advancement within the organization in search of status which also boosts self-esteem. For those who view work as a calling, money and status might still play a role, however, the main motivational factor is the work itself. The individual believes the work contributes to a greater purpose beyond self-interest. Such individuals experience higher gratification from work itself, and tend to report higher job and life satisfaction, as well as more meaning in life.

In Japan, the idea of having a purpose, a sense of calling in life, is called "Ikigai", which essentially means a reason to live or a reason to get up in the morning. Studies on blue zones, areas in the world with the highest rates of longevity, have found that a sense of purpose is a key ingredient in longevity and well-being. Knowing one's sense of purpose can increase life expectancy by up to seven years and decrease chances of suffering from Alzheimer's disease and stroke. Our purpose, our 'Ikigai' involves our passions, our strengths, and our values.

Aligning goals that focus our efforts and motivate us with our values and sense of calling provides us with a sense of direction and greater purpose in life. We now invite you to continue the journey by focusing on translating meaning into purpose and calling.

## Exercise 21: My Life is My Message

Gandhi once said: "My Life is My Message." What is yours?

To navigate through life, we need a sense of purpose which serves as a compass and guides our way. To begin this process, reflect on and write about the following questions:

1. What is your mission in life?

2. What kind of a person would you like to become?

3. How would you like to be remembered?

## Exercise 22: Building your Lighthouse

In this exercise you will 'build a lighthouse', or a personal mission statement. To do this, you will first consider what you want to be remembered for after your death and then, reflect on any potential regrets you may have. Using this information, you will create a personal mission statement (or lighthouse).

1) Begin with writing your own "Epitaph." What would you like to see inscribed on your tombstone? How would you best describe your life?

2) If you were going to die today, what will you regret not doing, saying, seeing or achieving?

3) Lastly, create a personal mission statement. Write a one paragraph statement that serves as a "lighthouse" to inspire

and guide your future actions. It should be simple, brief and positive. To find ingredients for your statement, please consider the personal strengths, values, and insights you have identified in previous exercises of this program (such as meaningful moments and choices). Also note, that your personal mission statement may change, as you might refine it on an ongoing basis throughout your life.

4) You could begin your statement, for example, by writing: "My mission in life is to XXXX. It is based upon my strengths of YYYY, passion for ZZZZ, and values of TTTTT."

## Exercise 23: Mooring your Life's Boat at the Shore of your Lighthouse

Make a plan - "Goals are dreams with deadlines" (Napoleon Hill).

Think about your typical week, how you usually spend your time: work, leisure, family, friends, etc.

Now consider your mission statement from the previous exercise:

A) How much of your mission statement is reflected in your typical week?

B) Which aspects of your mission statement are currently applied in your typical week?

C) Which aspects of your mission statement are missing from your typical week?

D) Commit yourself to three practical changes (small or big, as you wish) so that your mission statement is applied more fully in your typical week. These changes will allow you to live your purpose in everyday life more fully.

# Beyond Personal Meaning: Connecting with a Greater Cause

In essence, the key defining characteristics of meaning are connectedness and a contribution to something other than the self. This can be your family, or it can be nature, faith, or work. In other words, we can self-transcend, toward a person through love, caring, and relationships, and toward a cause that we find valuable and significant. As Frankl puts it, "being human means relating to something or someone other than oneself, be it a meaning to fulfill or a human being to encounter". Our existence falters and collapses until this self-transcending quality is lived out.

Psychological exploration, which is what you have been doing throughout this program, is a prerequisite to self-transcendence. If self-transcendence is the experience of moving beyond the self—that is, experiencing life from a place where we feel connected to everything and everyone—then, we need psychological exploration to get there. This is because it is extremely difficult to transcend that which we do not know or understand. Imagine that your personal self is like a jigsaw, and the different pieces of the puzzle come together to create a picture of our self. For us to self-transcend, that is, move beyond the experience of our own point of view, we need to learn and know how to recognize and work with the jigsaw pieces. That is why self-awareness is crucial. Only when we learn about the individual pieces of the puzzle, do we begin to learn what we are made of. Then we can let go and experience that self-transcendence, even if it is just a brief momentary experience.

In our everyday life, the emotions we feel are conditional, dependent upon our relationship with an event or a person. For example, when we are being told something nice by someone, it can be our boss telling us we've done a good job, we may feel happy. If we do not like our boss and he or she goes on vacation, we may feel peace. In both examples our emotions are conditional—that is, we feel an emotion as a result of something happening in our environment. In self-transcendence, however, the emotions we feel are unconditional, so when we move beyond that personal self, we feel unconditional love, peace, and happiness. These are not dependent upon anything that is happening in our environment. Mindfulness allows us to identify the conditions and requirements for the emotions, as we talked about earlier, and then let them go so that we can move on and experience more unconditional love, peace, and happiness.

When we transcend our individual selves and expand our view of the world, we begin to realize that in every situation in our lives, in every moment, lies a call to respond. A call to react in our own unique way. We are making our mark on a singular, unique moment in time. Such a subtle connection and partnership with life can be sensed when we pay close attention to life's gentle calling. It can be through the science of synchronicity or meaningful coincidence. It can be an inspirational song, a movie, or encounter that makes us feel that our lives have direction, purpose, and a mission or task. Frankl calls it "The unconscious God" in the depth of our being. Humans speak about a timeless, everlasting, yet fragile connection with the invisible. But in our hectic lives, we do not always find a time or an internal space to pause, to pay attention, to engage with this connection. One of the reasons for this may be explained by a phenomenon called 'hedonic adaptation.' Hedonic adaption means, once we experience positive feels after a new experience, after a while we get used to it and no longer experience the positive feelings. A beautiful scenery which we drive through, for example, might indeed be moving. But for people who live amongst the beautiful scenery may no longer see or appreciate the beauty, or be moved by it, as they have become used to it. Hedonic adaptation makes us less appreciative of everyday life and the meaning that it entails. When we practice seeing the sacred, the uniqueness of the mundane, we see it as scarce. With new eyes, a beginner's mind becomes like that of a child. We can train our minds to become more mindful of the meaning that exists all around us. When we pay attention, when we are attentive and present, we become conscious of life's gifts and miracles. Ralph Waldo Emerson once said, "if the stars should appear one night in a thousand years, how would men believe and adore and preserve for many generations the remembrance of the city of God, which has been shown, but every night come out those envoys of beauty and light the universe with their admonishing smile."

Mindfulness is required for both invitations into meaning within spirituality—to recognize the meaning of every moment—and for self-transcendence. For the former, by being mindful and looking at life as the miracle that it is, we are able to listen to and hear the whispers of meaning—the meaning potential that exists in each and every moment, each and every experience. Mindfulness becomes an incredible gift, allowing us all to be meaning detectives and become aware of the meaning that is infused in every moment in life. For self-transcendence, mindfulness is also required. Self-awareness is the foundation that takes us into self-transcendence, and mindfulness is the best tool for deepening self-awareness and self-knowledge. In other words, mindfulness takes us beyond personal meaning into an experience of meaning and purpose that deeply connects us with other people and anything else around us.

We now invite you to continue the journey by focusing on the theme of expanding beyond your personal meaning and connecting with the greater cause.

## Exercise 24: Loving-Kindness: A Path to Spiritual Meaning

You can download the meditation onto your computer or mobile phone and practice at any time that is convenient to you. Use this QR code to get this (free) meditation:

Alternatively, you can find the meditation script of the Loving-Kindness Meditation at the end of this workbook.

Practice at least once a day for a week. After completing each meditation practice (or at the end of the day), dedicate a few minutes to reflect on and answer the following questions:

- How was the practice of the loving-kindness meditation today? Did you notice anything?

- How did it feel to offer loving-kindness to yourself? Was there anything that surprised you in the experience?

## Exercise 25: Approaching Life with an Open Heart

Building on the former exercise of Loving-Kindness Meditation, you will now apply this quality in real-life.

We live in the little moments of life, not only in the "highs." As the old saying goes—"God is in the details." Today, you will sharpen your ability to notice and collect little moments of grace.

Start your day by practicing the Loving-Kindness Meditation. Approach it with a spirit of curiosity, openness, and freshness. Go through your day with an open heart, applying the loving-kindness attitude in your interactions with others (yes, even the challenging ones...). Do that with everything and everyone around you to elicit the grace and beauty that lies within you and the person or situation in front of you.

- What was it like to walk around with a sense of an open heart, loving-kindness and gratitude? Was it simple or challenging? If so, in what way?

- What impact, if any, did it have on your interactions with others, with the world, and with yourself today?

- What can you learn from this experience? What do you want to take from it?

## Exercise 26: The Extraordinary of the Ordinary

Read the following quote:

"Listen to your life. See it for the fathomless mystery that it is. In the boredom and pain of it no less than in the excitement and gladness: touch, taste, smell your way to the holy and hidden heart of it because in the last analysis all moments are key moments, and life itself is grace." - Frederick Buechner

- What do you feel/think while reading this quote? (e.g., in your body, thoughts, emotions, memories, insights…).

- Can you recall such an experience of the grace of life, finding the sacred within the mundane (e.g., with nature/a relationship…)?

- How did it feel when this happened?

## Exercise 27: An Attitude of the Sacred

You will now choose a mundane activity and approach it with mindfulness and an attitude of the sacred. You are going to apply the spirit of the quote you read in the previous exercise. You can choose any of your everyday activities. For example, taking a shower, speaking to your partner, playing with your child, walking in the park/street. Whatever activity you choose, make sure that you find that quality of mindfulness and holiness as part of your relationship with the experience. At the end of the day, or immediately following completion of the exercise, answer these questions:

- What everyday experience did you choose for this exercise?

- How did it feel applying mindfulness and the sacred to the experience?

- Did it feel different compared with previous times? If so, in what way?

# Mindfulness and Meaning: Bringing it all Together

During this program, we have covered the following topics: we explored what is meant by meaning, which is essentially the feeling that our lives matter, are coherent, and are directed toward a purpose or broader mission. We offered an in-depth understanding of mindfulness, including its definition, the benefits, the experience of it, and myths that surround it. Next, we explored our life story to gain a deeper understanding of meaningful events, choices, and sources of meaning, as well as the importance of finding meaning in the present moment and the experience of presence, how it leads us into savoring, and the way it leads to a deep feeling of meaning in the here and now. We also discussed the importance of having a sense of direction, purpose, and calling as a reason to get up in the morning and how we can translate our purpose into self-concordant goals. We then offered an exploration of meaning beyond the personal level. We talked about an experience of meaning that is based on a deep connection to other people and other sources of meaning that went beyond the individual.

As this journey approaches its destination, it is important to discuss the relevance of regular practice and how impactful this is when it comes to the results of this program. Research indicates that people who continue the practice not only during the program but also afterwards, find it much more beneficial. The impact of the program increases, and at some point, is no longer a practice, but instead becomes a part of who you are. This is where the idea that with practice comes change that can be very clearly seen.

We also need to highlight that meaning and purpose might change. Sometimes, people say that they had a meaningful experience in life, and they thought—this is it. I will just stay here for the remainder of my life, but then at some point life felt empty. Whether it was a certain person or some situation or a job or whatever, they no longer feel relevant or meaningful anymore. We invite you to let go of the image of meaning and purpose being a heavy rock. They do not sit there unchanged, throughout time. Instead, think about them as a river that flows and changes, because life itself is changing and you are changing. You may be familiar with the saying that you cannot step into the same river twice. Likewise, meaning and purpose are fluid. Moving and changing, being aware of ourselves, then becomes a crucial daily task. Because when you are aware of yourself, you are aware of the subtle changes in meaning and purpose, and you can readjust your choices, your way of being, everything that you are, and whatever you find in relation to your meaning and purpose.

We invite you to choose the exercise that has been most impactful for you throughout this program and practice it for at least a few weeks. When that exercise feels less relevant, go back to the list of exercises, choose a different one, and practice it for a while. This kind of self-awareness work ends with our last breath. If we believe self-awareness is essential to our growth, then we will learn something new and develop further each time we do an exercise. Richard Bach once said, "how would you know whether your mission upon earth has ended? As long as you are alive, it didn't end." The experience you have gone through as part of this program is just the beginning of the journey. We hope that doors have been opened and opportunities have now opened up within you. And that this is just the beginning of an inward journey where the meaning and purpose becomes clear.

Thank you for your dedication, your courage, and your self-engagement throughout this journey. We wish you a continued life of adventures filled with inspiration and passion, and deep, deep meaning and purpose.

## Exercise 28: Back Home from Your Journey: A Reflection

Review the exercises you have completed throughout this workbook and choose the 10 exercises that were most meaningful and transformative for you. Once those 10 are chosen, create a visual reminder for each of them. It can be a photo, a drawing, an on-line visual or a doodle. Now, on a large white board, paper, or cardboard, glue or pin each of these images so that they tell the story and outline the map of your journey.

Once completed, observe your creation closely:

- What stands out for you?

- What insights do you have?

- How does your newly-created image make you feel?

## Exercise 29: Life after the Journey: Practical Insights for a Meaning-Filled Life

1. Looking back at the goal you set at the beginning of the program, was it fulfilled?

2. What are the three things you got out of the program but did not expect to?

3. How will you implement what you have learned as part of the program in your everyday life?

4. Is there anything you need to implement these insights? (e.g., support from others, structured daily schedule, new habits…) Try to be as specific as possible.

# Exercise 30: Making it Stick: Creating Habits of Mindful Meaning

Go back and review all of the exercises you have practiced as part of the program.

Choose the exercise that feels most relevant to you right now and practice it a couple of times during the week. Once you feel it is no longer relevant, choose another exercise and practice it a couple of times during the week. If you come across a different exercise outside of this program, but is relevant to your meaning and purpose, you can switch and practice this instead.

Remember, personal growth requires the cultivation of self-awareness. When you practice, you water and nourish the seeds of transformation within yourself.

# Guided Meditation Scripts

## 1. Breathing Meditation

Welcome to this 5-minute breathing meditation …

Make sure you're in a comfortable position, and all of your clothes are loose around the waist to allow for

easy breathing … you may close your eyes if you wish ….

begin to draw in a long and slow deep breath… and hold it at the top for just a moment … then release….

good …. breathe in deeply and slowly once again … hold it … and let it go …. nice ….

the breath is a powerful tool for relaxation that we all have access to at any moment in our life … so really

allow yourself to be relaxed by the breath … imagine that you are breathing in peace and calm … inhaling

… and when you breathe out, the diaphragm relaxes and so do you …. breathing in tranquility … hold it ….

and breathe out relaxing ….

keep your focus on the breath ….

breathing in deeply …. and breathe out into relaxation ….

by maintaining concentration on the breath even when your thoughts stray, you are practicing the art of meditation … it's perfectly fine if you have interruptive thoughts coming in … soon as you notice, just

return your thoughts to the breath… breathing in that peace and breathing out into relaxation ….. good

…

Now we are going to count as we breathe …. on the in breath, you count one, and on the out breath two

… on the next in breath it will be 3, and when you breathe out, 4 … I will guide you …go ahead breathe in

deeply, 1 …. And breathe out, 2… breathe in, 3… breathing out, 4… breathing in, 5… breathing out, 6….

Breathe in, 7… and breathe out, 8… one more, breathe in, 9 and breathe out, 10….

Become aware of your level of relaxation right now…

in times of stress or worry, if you consciously breathe, you can find that you will relax…. and if you need a

little extra support, simply count along with the breaths, in whatever way feels comfortable for you…

So, let's take one more last deep breath in together… breathing in, filling your lungs as much as you can…

and when you breathe out, open your eyes, ready to return to your day with confidence.

## 2. Body Scan Meditation

Welcome to this relaxing body scan focus meditation …

doing a body scan is a great way to place your attention on your body and put you in the present

moment … allowing you to feel relaxed and focused … let's begin draw your attention to the very Top of your head … you may notice your hair or lack thereof … you could

be wearing a hat … whatever you notice just become aware of it and place all of your focus on the very

Top of your head … good …

now draw your focus to the very tip of your nose … all of

your attention on the tip of the nose … perhaps you can

feel the air coming in and out gently … nice …

now drawing your focus to the fingertips …

Noticing how your fingertips feel right now … no need to do anything just place your awareness on the

fingertips ….

wonderful …

now bring your attention to the toes … are they warm or are they cool … are you wearing socks or are

you barefoot …

place all of your awareness on your toes … wonderful …

now drawing your attention to the belly, the abdomen … notice how it rises and falls along with the breath

… lovely …

now let's bring our attention to the neck … if you have any tension here let it simply melt away, you

don't need it right now …

and now the shoulders … all of your focus here on the shoulders …

allow for them to drop down a little bit more, relaxing … very good …

and now focus on your legs .... focusing on both of your legs at the same time ... nice

.... and now both of your arms, all of your attention on your arms ... great ...

and now your entire back ... place all of your focus on your spine and muscles of the back ... awesome ...

a body scan is a wonderful way to focus your attention as well as relax you more and more the longer

you do it. so practice this technique daily and notice how your focusing abilities increase.

## 3. Gratitude Meditation

Hello and welcome to this meditation on gratitude...

Adjust your position so that you are relaxed and all of your muscles can let go...You can move at any time

during this session in order to give you maximum comfort. Allow your eyes to gently close.

Take a big deep breath in and out.

Take another breath in and bring into your mind the feeling of gratitude.

Now notice, where in your body is the feeling of gratitude expressed? Do you feel it rise in your heart?

Perhaps your abdomen... Wherever you feel these sensations, study the quality of them. Are they subtle

or not so subtle?

You may feel grateful for something you have... bring into your mind those objects you are grateful for, such as your house and your bed. Breathe deeply into your thoughts as you imagine these things. As you

exhale, whisper to yourself, "thank you."

Express gratitude for those you know… allow this person, people and even animals to rise in your mind…

see them clearly, breathe deeply into your imagination, perhaps you can even hear how they sound. As

you breathe out, whisper to yourself, "thank you."

Become grateful for yourself. Your health, your wisdom, your kindness. Be grateful for those times you

stood up for yourself, or for someone else. Be grateful for your ability to love others. Breathe in deeply,

imagining that you can give yourself a big hug, and whisper, "thank you."

Now express gratitude even for the smallest things… whatever small things pop in your mind now, be

grateful for them… Breathe in again, feeling the importance of even the little things, and exhale,

whispering to yourself, "thank you."

Take a nice breath in and be grateful for your breath… bringing you life. letting your

breath go, your body sinking deeper into relaxation.

Practice the art of gratitude little by little.

Gracious… Grateful… Gratitude… Whenever you are ready, rise from your meditation and open your eyes.

# 4. Mindful Meaning in Challenge

I invite you to sit comfortably. Have you back straight. That your hands rest on your thighs or knees and close your eyes. Begin by inhaling and exhaling fully. As you inhale, bring your full awareness into your body. As you exhale let the body soften. Relax. You are signaling to your brain that you are now shifting into an alternative state of consciousness.

One in which you are fully engaged, connected to the here and now within you. Inhaling deep awareness, exhaling softness. Keep your back straight so that the body's alert in a way, while at the same time letting your shoulders soften, relax. the eyebrows relax, the cheekbones surrender and the jaw softens. Now, deliberately bring to mind a challenging situation that is going on in your life at the moment.

Something you don't mind staying with for a few minutes. Please don't choose something too traumatic. Just a mild challenge. Something that is currently unresolved. Allow the challenging situation to rest in your mind, that you are willing to experience the challenge for a minute. Might trigger certain discomfort. Let it be triggered, as long as it is bearable. As long as you can contain it.

Once you are fully engaged with the challenge, shift your attention into your body so that you become aware of the physical sensations. Feelings that accompany the thoughts and emotions relating to your challenge.

Bring your full attention to the area in the body where the sensation is strongest. You can use your breath as a vehicle to go there into that place where you can feel something most strongly. Breathe into that space in your body.

You are not trying to change the sensation you simply observe it, becoming aware of it. Silently, compassionately say to yourself, it's okay to feel this. It's okay to be open to this.

It's okay to feel this. It's okay to be open to this. Breath in to that part of the body where you feel the sensation. Say to yourself, it is here now. It's okay to feel this. It's already here. Let me open up to it. If possible, let go of any tensing and bracing. Soften and open up to these sensations.

Say to yourself, softening as you inhale and opening as you exhale. Inhale softening. Exhale opening. Softening, opening. Now that you are fully engaged from within with your challenging situation. I invite you to find the meaning and purpose of that challenge for you.

Take your time and allow the answer to appear in your mind. Ask yourself, why have I experienced that challenge? What meaning and purpose is it serving in my life?

What meaning and purpose is it serving in my life? Make sure you're not carried away into any stories or other thoughts. Keep your mind very, very focused on the challenge itself and its meaning for you.

Take a minute to imprint in your consciousness the insight of the meaning and purpose you have found for that challenge.

Once you feel the meaning is clear within you, bring your awareness back to your whole body and gently, gradually, let your eyes open.

## 5. Best possible Legacy Meditation

Welcome to the Daily Meditation for Session six. This session will focus on becoming more aware of the things in life we find most meaningful. I invite you to be curious, kind and accepting as you're guided through this process. To begin meditating, I would like to invite you to sit comfortably, adjust your posture so that you're sitting in any upright position with your spine straight, let your eyes close, relax your shoulders, soften your jaw, and let go of any tension in your body.

Take a couple of deep, full inhales and exhale fully releasing all of the stale air from your lungs. Inhale fresh oxygen and exhale fully. Do that a few more times.

Focus your awareness on your breath. Use your breath as an anchor to your awareness. Putting your awareness again and again to the experience of breathing. The experience of presence here, now, with your breath. As you inhale, allow your awareness to follow your breath. Moving into the body. As you exhale allow your body to relax. Inhale awareness. Exhale relaxation.

As you inhale. Feel the air coming in touch with your nostrils and nose, throat chest and lungs. And as you exhale, soften your body, soften your muscles while maintaining a straight spine. As you watch your breath, continue to concentrate and the sensations in your body. If at any point you find your mind wandering, simply notice that it has wandered.

Let the thoughts go and gently bring your mind back to the breath. From this place of relaxation begin to visualize yourself in the future. Take yourself to a place in time where you see yourself living a meaningful life. You have achieved everything you wish to achieve and have done everything you set out to do. Visualize a scenario that illustrates vividly this meaningful life.

Imagine people you meet, interactions, situations, anything else that embodies what you visualize as a most meaningful life for you. This future vision of yourself is the best possible legacy you could leave behind. Breathe deeply and connect fully to the experience.

Try not to hold on to any thoughts about how you got there. Simply imagine it as vividly as you can and feel the emotions this vision evokes.

Take all the time you need to visualize all aspects of this future life. Breathe and observe. Gradually shift from imagining your best possible legacy to the actual sensations that are triggered in your body. Bring your awareness into your body. Feel the sensations that arise in your body as you witness the experience of living a meaningful life. Breathe in and out.

Scan your body and find the most prominent sensations. Breath in to these sensations. Feel and explore them. Do nothing about these sensations. Simply observe. Breathe. Witness. Do you find that your mind has wandered to a thought, an image, an idea, immediately with a smiling attitude bring it back to the sensations in your body.

These bodily sensations arise from contemplating your meaningful life. Notice what you are feeling in your body. Appreciate the sensations you notice. Watch them with kindness. Watch them with acceptance. I invite you now to deepen your breath and bring your awareness to your whole body. Feel the environment around you. The sound of my voice. Your presence. My presence. Our presence.

Take as much time as you want and when you feel ready, you can slowly open your eyes.

# 6. Loving-Kindness Meditation

Find a comfortable position preferably lying down so that you can become fully relaxed.

**Sit comfortably. Any position will do.** Close your eyes and take a few deep breaths. Inhale and exhale slowly and consciously relax your muscles and prepare body and mind for deep awareness of love and compassion.

**Choose a person you love.** Choose someone who you love easily and naturally rather than someone for whom you feel an emotionally complicated love.

**Focus on the area around your heart.** Put your hand over your heart. Once you are able to focus on your heart, imagine breathing in and out through your heart. Take several deep breaths and feel your heart breathing.

**Turn your attention to feelings of gratitude and love**, warm and tender feelings, for the person you chose.

**Send Loving-Kindness and Compassion to Yourself:** Imagine that the warm glow of love and compassion coming from your heart is moving throughout your body. Send these feelings up and down your body. If verbal content is easier for you to connect to, you can repeat the following words: May I be happy. May I be well. May I be safe. May I be peaceful and at ease.

**Send Loving-Kindness and Compassion to Family and Friends:** Imagine friends and family as vividly as you can, and send these feelings into their hearts. Imagine the warm glow of love and compassion that comes from your heart moving into their hearts. If verbal content is easier for you to connect to, you can repeat the following words: May you be happy. May you be well. May you be safe. May you be peaceful and at ease.

**Expand the circle** by sending your Loving-Kindness and Compassion to neighbours, acquaintances, strangers, animals, and finally people with whom you have difficulty.

**Imagine planet earth, with all of its inhabitants,** and send Loving-Kindness and Compassion to all living beings.

# About the Authors

**Dr. Pninit Russo-Netzer** is passionate about building bridges – between disciplines and between theory and "real life" practice, in therapy, organizations, communities, and education throughout the lifespan. She is a senior lecturer and researcher, a logotherapist, and the founder and head of the Academic Training Program for Logotherapy (meaning-oriented psychotherapy) at Tel-Aviv University. She is also the head of the Education Department at Achva Academic College, and the head of the 'Compass' Institute for the Study and Application of Meaning in life. She serves as academic advisor and consultant to both academic and non-academic institutions, and develops training programs and curricula for various organizations on positive psychology, logotherapy, leadership, meaning in life, resilience and spirituality worldwide. She has published numerous academic articles and chapters and is the coauthor of five books and co-editor of four books on the topics of meaning in life, positive psychology, existential psychology, positive change and growth.

**Dr. Itai Ivtzan** is passionate about the combination of Positive Psychology and Mindfulness. It makes his heart sing. He is convinced that if we befriend both of those practices and succeed in introducing them into our lives, we will all become super-heroes and gain super-strengths of awareness, courage, resilience, and compassion. Isn't this an amazing prospect? Dr. Itai Ivtzan is a positive psychologist, a Professor at Naropa University, and the School of Positive Transformation Director. Over the past 20 years, Dr. Ivtzan has run seminars, lectures, workshops, and retreats in the USA, UK, and worldwide, at various educational institutions and private events. He is a regular keynote speaker at conferences. He published five books and more than 50 journal papers and book chapters. His main areas of research and teaching are positive psychology, mindfulness, and spirituality. As part of his work, he established the School of Positive Transformation, offering practical Well-being courses for practitioners, teaching them how to transform themselves and their clients and students.